This journal is about making some time for yourself. where you get to think, create, and explore your dreams for the year ahead. How you choose to to you. It's not dated, so you can begin whe tailor it to suit your needs. Whether you h creative projects, personal goals, or a co these pages give you the space to explore

There is a 52-week planner, with space for long-t goals and objectives; 13 four-week planners, helping you to break those goals down into achievable tasks; and 52 weekly planner and reflection pages, where you can write your tasks, and review your week. We've added prompts to guide you, lined boxes to fill, blank areas to doodle in, and quotes to inspire. There's space to review your progress as you go, and to record your thoughts, feelings, and special moments. Feel free to write, draw, paste in photos, or embellish your journal in any way you see fit. It's your space to reflect on those things you rarely have time for, and all you hope to become.

The editors of Breathe Magazine

WEEKLY REFLECTION PROMPTS

Try setting aside time each week to think about what's working for you, what isn't, and what needs changing. Plus, there are all those special moments in life that can so easily be forgotten if you don't write them down. Here are a few questions and ideas you could ponder as each of the next 52 weeks unfolds. Write, draw, or doodle the thoughts they bring to mind

Things that raised a smile

The best hour of the week was when. . .

I have learned. . .

Little things that brought me joy

I love that I managed to. . .

What was the biggest obstacle I overcame?

What did I learn from a positive experience?

What did I learn from a negative experience?

If I were to sum up this week in a sketch

If I were to sum up this week in a sentence

What surprised me this week

I was inspired most by. . .

Emotionally, I was affected by. . .

My stressful situations— small and large

Who was important to me?

What was my most meaningful conversation?

Did I go outside my comfort zone? How?

This week was memorable because. . .

I was motivated by. . .

My spirits were lifted by. . .

I overcame my fear of. . .

The person who inspired me most was. . .

I helped others by. . .

The person who made
a significant difference

I roared laughing when. . .

The most significant
moment was. . .

I conquered my self-
doubt by. . .

I felt strong when. . .

I felt challenged when. . .

I felt proud when. . .

I dreamed about. . .

Changes I want to make

My energy was drained by. . .

What made me feel sad?

What made me feel good?

I took a step forward in. . .

What do I want to
leave behind?

Did any quotes speak
to my heart?

If I'd had an extra day,
I would have. . .

At the moment, I love. . .

I'm grateful that. . .

Thoughts I want to keep

Inner doubts I'd like
to shake off

A joke or nice phrase I heard

How could the week
have been improved?

What I want to remember

I wish I'd acted
differently when. . .

A real positive was. . .

My favorite word or
saying right now is. . .

*Write down other prompts
that are important to
you in the boxes below:*

52-WEEK PLAN

*Start your journey with these questions (and your answers)
in mind and it might help you to realize ambitions, make
changes, and plan for the future*

What are my goals?

to create — be more playful
live The moment/present +
Think what is The best/what
I am grateful

What are my dreams?

Keep my inner strenght
Keep my peace, hope + faith

What is my motivation?

be grateful to conquer
any obstacle and leave
The present to cheer it

How do I want to feel?

Peaceful / Hopeful/

What or who do I need for support?

Prayer, friends, husband

How can I make a difference?

Leave The moment
Being grateful

What do I want to learn?

NOT to worry when
I cant control / Trust
THINK POSITIVE

What can I let go?

Sadness / worry

Which new activity would I like to try?

Read, Draw, learn some
Thing every day.

Where do I want to explore?

Places close by

How can I demonstrate kindness?

Control of sadness or
worrys

How can I be more mindful?

Leave every moment

notes

How can I take better care of my physical and mental health?

do exercise

Which habit would I like to work into my routine?

excersise   laugh
ceramic
read
pray

How can I bring more positive energy into my life?

play with activities
relax

How can I reward myself?

love my self

4-WEEK PLAN

| JAN | FEB | MAR | APR | MAY | JUN | JUL | AUG | SEP | OCT | NOV | DEC |

WEEKLY PLANNER

M
to wake up early
prayed / finish pmts
did ceramic / relax
after stress / swimming

T

W
hice moldes !!
vi a Fercito !!
Hable con Sol y Evy

T

F

S

S

TRACKER	M	T	W	T	F	S	S

WEEKLY PLANNER

M

T

W

T Busco sentirme bien
Dejar preocupaciones
No afectarme de nada

F

S

S

Si tomo tiempo
para mi voy
a sentirme
mejor.
Agradecer ,
cada sensación
y momento
Si llega algo
triste, soltarlo

TRACKER	M	T	W	T	F	S	S

WEEKLY PLANNER

M

T

W

T

F

S

S

TRACKER	M	T	W	T	F	S	S

WEEKLY PLANNER

M

T

W

T

F

S

S

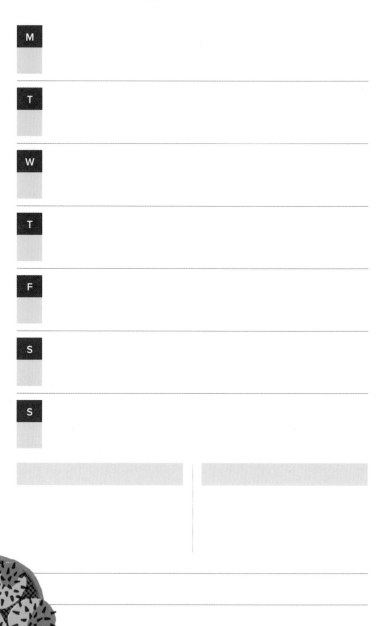

TRACKER	M	T	W	T	F	S	S

WEEKLY NOTES

"We always may be what we might have been"

ADELAIDE ANNE PROCTER

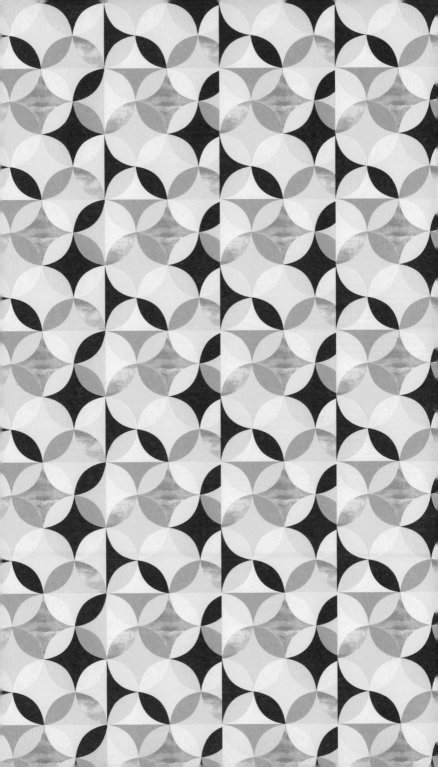

4-WEEK PLAN

| JAN | FEB | MAR | APR | MAY | JUN | JUL | AUG | SEP | OCT | NOV | DEC |

WEEKLY PLANNER

M

T

W

T

F

S

S

TRACKER	M	T	W	T	F	S	S

WEEKLY PLANNER

M

T

W

T

F

S

S

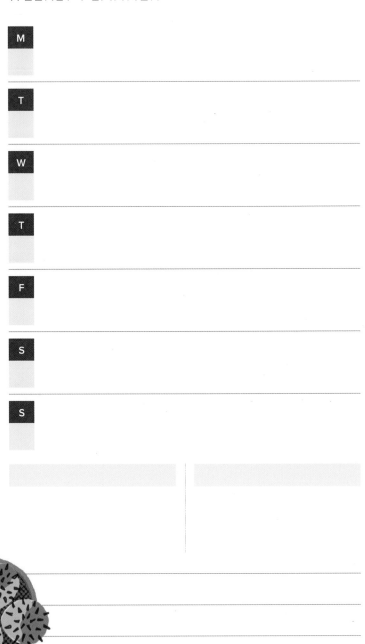

TRACKER	M	T	W	T	F	S	S

WEEKLY PLANNER

M

T

W

T

F

S

S

WEEKLY REFLECTION

TRACKER	M	T	W	T	F	S	S

WEEKLY PLANNER

M

T

W

T

F

S

S

TRACKER	M	T	W	T	F	S	S

WEEKLY NOTES

"The best way to predict your future is to create it"

ABRAHAM LINCOLN

4-WEEK PLAN

JAN FEB MAR APR MAY JUN JUL AUG SEP OCT NOV DEC

WEEKLY PLANNER

M

T

W

T

F

S

S

WEEKLY REFLECTION

TRACKER	M	T	W	T	F	S	S

WEEKLY PLANNER

M

T

W

T

F

S

S

TRACKER	M	T	W	T	F	S	S

WEEKLY PLANNER

M

T

W

T

F

S

S

WEEKLY REFLECTION

TRACKER	M	T	W	T	F	S	S

WEEKLY PLANNER

M

T

W

T

F

S

S

TRACKER	M	T	W	T	F	S	S

WEEKLY NOTES

"Don't cry because it's over, smile
because it happened"

DR. SEUSS

4-WEEK PLAN

| JAN | FEB | MAR | APR | MAY | JUN | JUL | AUG | SEP | OCT | NOV | DEC |

WEEKLY PLANNER

M

T

W

T

F

S

S

TRACKER	M	T	W	T	F	S	S

WEEKLY PLANNER

M

T

W

T

F

S

S

TRACKER	M	T	W	T	F	S	S

WEEKLY PLANNER

M

T

W

T

F

S

S

TRACKER	M	T	W	T	F	S	S

WEEKLY PLANNER

M

T

W

T

F

S

S

TRACKER	M	T	W	T	F	S	S

WEEKLY NOTES

"Life is a great big canvas; throw all
the paint on it you can"

DANNY KAYE

4-WEEK PLAN

JAN FEB MAR APR MAY JUN JUL AUG SEP OCT NOV DEC

WEEKLY PLANNER

M

T

W

T

F

S

S

TRACKER	M	T	W	T	F	S	S

WEEKLY PLANNER

M

T

W

T

F

S

S

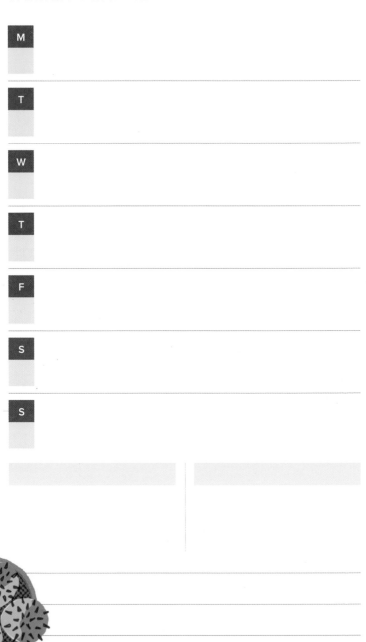

WEEKLY REFLECTION

TRACKER	M	T	W	T	F	S	S

WEEKLY PLANNER

M

T

W

T

F

S

S

TRACKER	M	T	W	T	F	S	S

WEEKLY PLANNER

M

T

W

T

F

S

S

WEEKLY REFLECTION

TRACKER	M	T	W	T	F	S	S

WEEKLY NOTES

"If you don't like the road you're walking,
start paving another one"

DOLLY PARTON

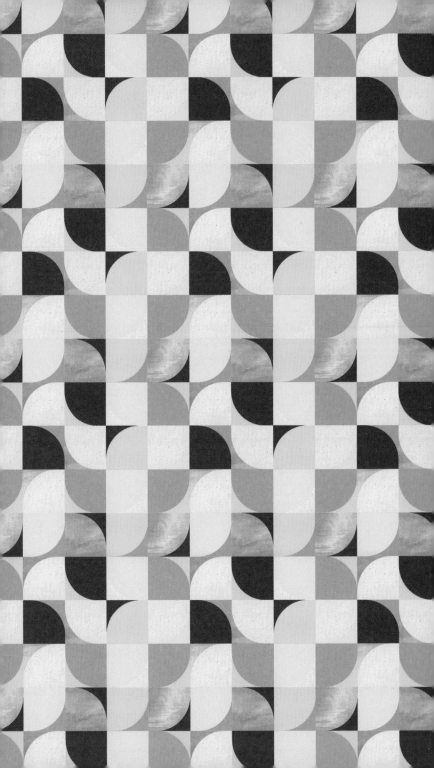

4-WEEK PLAN

JAN FEB MAR APR MAY JUN JUL AUG SEP OCT NOV DEC

WEEKLY PLANNER

M

T

W

T

F

S

S

WEEKLY REFLECTION

TRACKER	M	T	W	T	F	S	S

WEEKLY PLANNER

M

T

W

T

F

S

S

TRACKER	M	T	W	T	F	S	S

WEEKLY PLANNER

M

T

W

T

F

S

S

TRACKER	M	T	W	T	F	S	S

WEEKLY PLANNER

M

T

W

T

F

S

S

WEEKLY REFLECTION

TRACKER	M	T	W	T	F	S	S

WEEKLY NOTES

"Great things are done by a series of small
things brought together"

VINCENT VAN GOGH

4-WEEK PLAN

JAN | FEB | MAR | APR | MAY | JUN | JUL | AUG | SEP | OCT | NOV | DEC

WEEKLY PLANNER

M

T

W

T

F

S

S

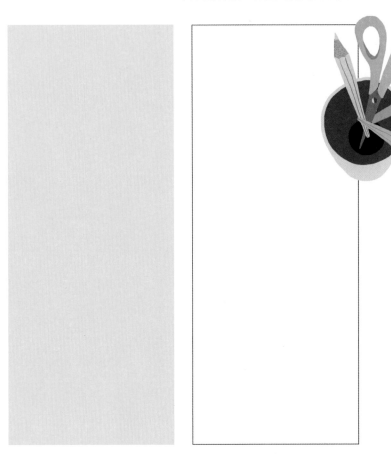

TRACKER	M	T	W	T	F	S	S

WEEKLY PLANNER

M

T

W

T

F

S

S

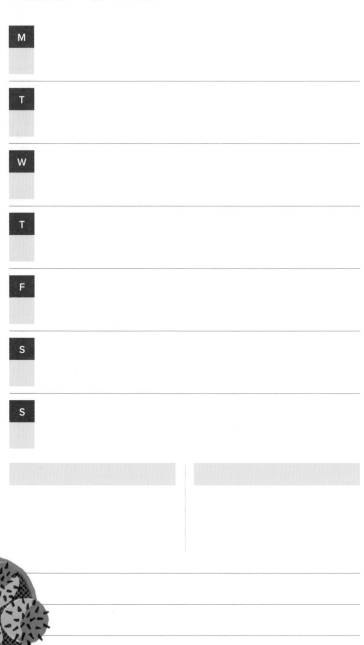

TRACKER	M	T	W	T	F	S	S

WEEKLY PLANNER

M

T

W

T

F

S

S

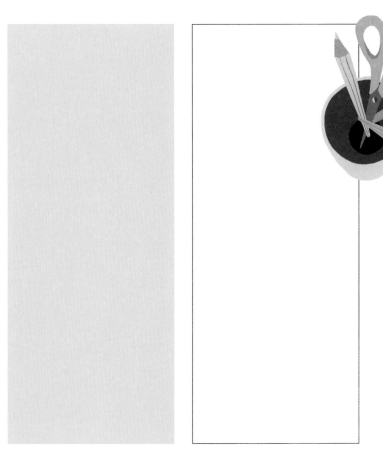

WEEKLY REFLECTION

TRACKER	M	T	W	T	F	S	S

WEEKLY PLANNER

M

T

W

T

F

S

S

TRACKER	M	T	W	T	F	S	S

WEEKLY NOTES

"The biggest adventure you can take is to
live the life of your dreams"

OPRAH WINFREY

4-WEEK PLAN

| JAN | FEB | MAR | APR | MAY | JUN | JUL | AUG | SEP | OCT | NOV | DEC |

WEEKLY PLANNER

M

T

W

T

F

S

S

TRACKER	M	T	W	T	F	S	S

WEEKLY PLANNER

M

T

W

T

F

S

S

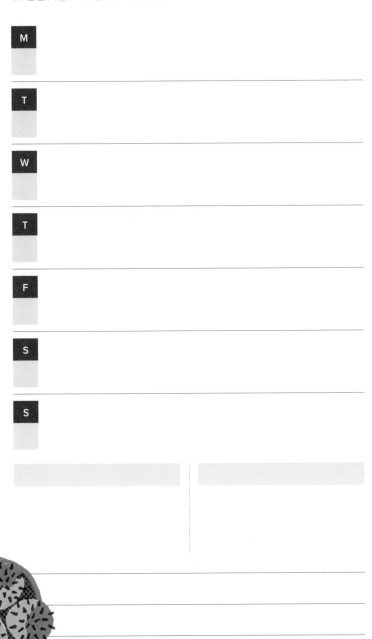

TRACKER	M	T	W	T	F	S	S

WEEKLY PLANNER

M

T

W

T

F

S

S

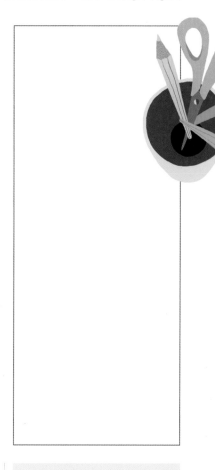

TRACKER	M	T	W	T	F	S	S

WEEKLY PLANNER

M

T

W

T

F

S

S

TRACKER	M	T	W	T	F	S	S

WEEKLY NOTES

"All life is an experiment. The more experiments
you make the better"

RALPH WALDO EMERSON

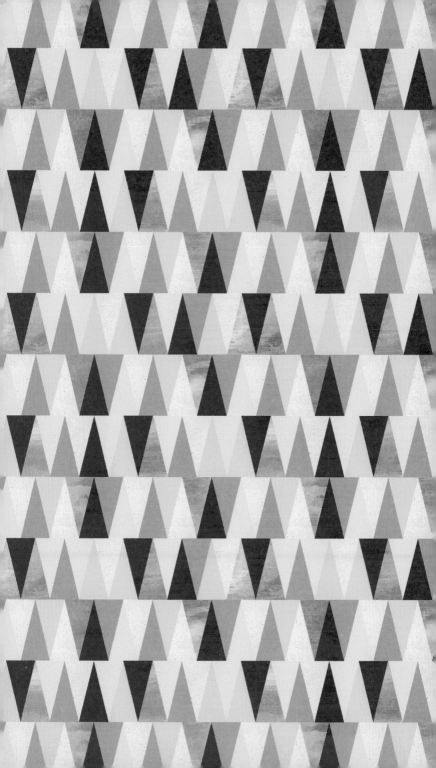

4-WEEK PLAN

JAN FEB MAR APR MAY JUN JUL AUG SEP OCT NOV DEC

WEEKLY PLANNER

M

T

W

T

F

S

S

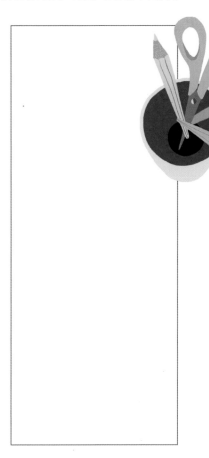

TRACKER	M	T	W	T	F	S	S

WEEKLY PLANNER

M

T

W

T

F

S

S

TRACKER	M	T	W	T	F	S	S

WEEKLY PLANNER

M

T

W

T

F

S

S

WEEKLY REFLECTION

TRACKER	M	T	W	T	F	S	S

WEEKLY PLANNER

M

T

W

T

F

S

S

WEEKLY REFLECTION

TRACKER	M	T	W	T	F	S	S

WEEKLY NOTES

"It is the sweet, simple things of life which
are the real ones after all".

LAURA INGALLS WILDER

4-WEEK PLAN

| JAN | FEB | MAR | APR | MAY | JUN | JUL | AUG | SEP | OCT | NOV | DEC |

WEEKLY PLANNER

M

T

W

T

F

S

S

TRACKER	M	T	W	T	F	S	S

WEEKLY PLANNER

M

T

W

T

F

S

S

TRACKER	M	T	W	T	F	S	S

WEEKLY PLANNER

M

T

W

T

F

S

S

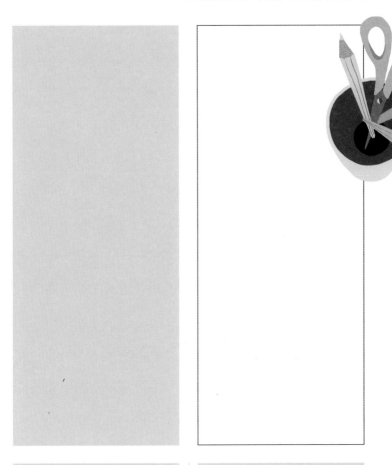

TRACKER	M	T	W	T	F	S	S

WEEKLY PLANNER

M

T

W

T

F

S

S

TRACKER	M	T	W	T	F	S	S

WEEKLY NOTES

"I've failed over and over and over again
in my life and that is why I succeed"

MICHAEL JORDAN

4-WEEK PLAN

| JAN | FEB | MAR | APR | MAY | JUN | JUL | AUG | SEP | OCT | NOV | DEC |

WEEKLY PLANNER

M

T

W

T

F

S

S

TRACKER	M	T	W	T	F	S	S

WEEKLY PLANNER

M

T

W

T

F

S

S

WEEKLY REFLECTION

TRACKER	M	T	W	T	F	S	S

WEEKLY PLANNER

M

T

W

T

F

S

S

WEEKLY REFLECTION

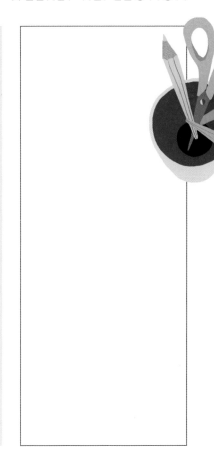

TRACKER	M	T	W	T	F	S	S

WEEKLY PLANNER

M

T

W

T

F

S

S

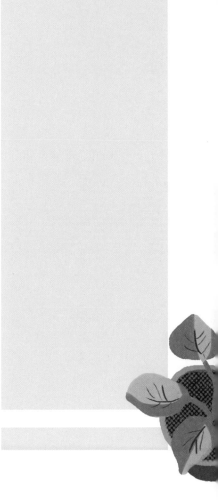

TRACKER	M	T	W	T	F	S	S

WEEKLY NOTES

"Motivation comes from working on
things we care about"

4-WEEK PLAN

JAN · FEB · MAR · APR · MAY · JUN · JUL · AUG · SEP · OCT · NOV · DEC

WEEKLY PLANNER

M

T

W

T

F

S

S

WEEKLY REFLECTION

TRACKER	M	T	W	T	F	S	S

WEEKLY PLANNER

M

T

W

T

F

S

S

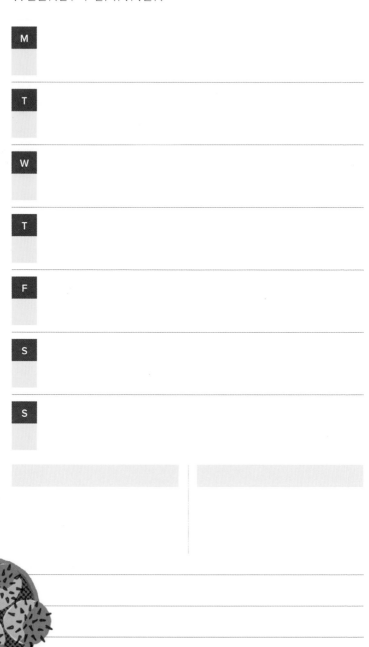

WEEKLY REFLECTION

TRACKER	M	T	W	T	F	S	S

WEEKLY PLANNER

M

T

W

T

F

S

S

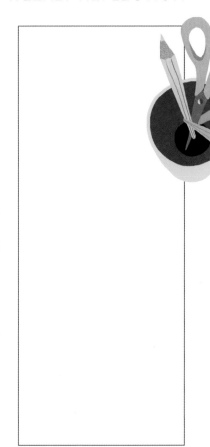

TRACKER	M	T	W	T	F	S	S

WEEKLY PLANNER

M

T

W

T

F

S

S

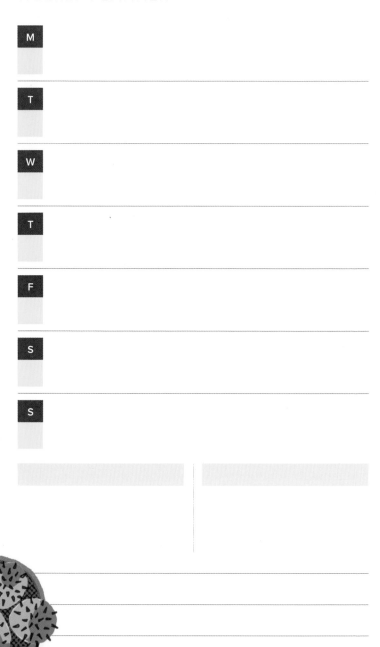

TRACKER	M	T	W	T	F	S	S

WEEKLY NOTES

"Don't wait. The time will never be just right"

4-WEEK PLAN

JAN	FEB	MAR	APR	MAY	JUN	JUL	AUG	SEP	OCT	NOV	DEC

WEEKLY PLANNER

M

T

W

T

F

S

S

WEEKLY REFLECTION

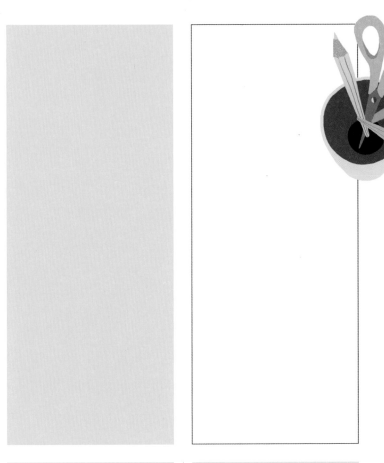

TRACKER	M	T	W	T	F	S	S

WEEKLY PLANNER

M

T

W

T

F

S

S

TRACKER	M	T	W	T	F	S	S

WEEKLY PLANNER

M

T

W

T

F

S

S

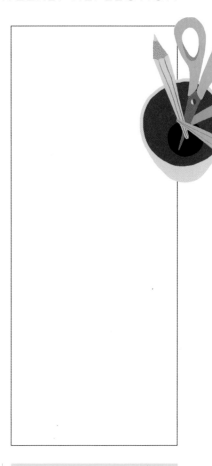

TRACKER	M	T	W	T	F	S	S

WEEKLY PLANNER

M

T

W

T

F

S

S

TRACKER	M	T	W	T	F	S	S

WEEKLY NOTES

"Do the best you can until you know better.
Then when you know better, do better"

MAYA ANGELOU

52-WEEK PLAN REVIEW

Exploring the good, the less good, and the in-between can set you on a more fulfilling path for the future...

Which goals did you achieve and which goals eluded you? What made some possible and which areas were tricky?

....

....

....

Did any of your dreams come true? Did they bring you the joy you thought they would? Are your dreams as important now as they were, or have any of them changed?

....

....

....

Were your motivations sound and did they remain constant? Did you recognize the progress you made as you went along?

....

....

....

Do your feelings now reflect what you anticipated or hoped?

....

....

....

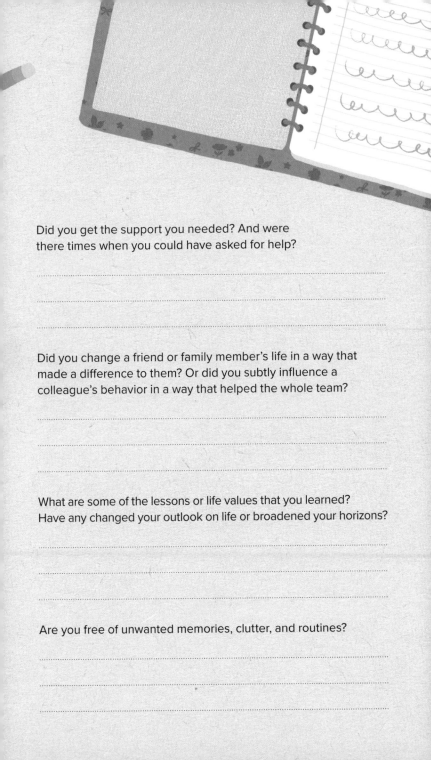

Did you get the support you needed? And were there times when you could have asked for help?

....

....

....

Did you change a friend or family member's life in a way that made a difference to them? Or did you subtly influence a colleague's behavior in a way that helped the whole team?

....

....

....

What are some of the lessons or life values that you learned? Have any changed your outlook on life or broadened your horizons?

....

....

....

Are you free of unwanted memories, clutter, and routines?

....

....

....

Did you get to try a new activity? Did you enjoy it and how might you take it further? If it wasn't what you'd hoped, list other hobbies you could think about trying.

....

....

....

Was there time to explore the places you wanted to? Or was your exploration more psychological? What did you learn?

....

....

....

Did you find ways to show kindness and who benefitted from your actions? How did it make you feel?

....

....

....

Were you more mindful? In what ways? Did you notice your surroundings more or the colors and textures of life?
Explore how you felt about them.

....

....

....

Was there time to think more about your physical and mental health and look after yourself? If not, try to think about why and ways that you might change the situation.

....

....

....

Does your routine reflect a new habit? Has it changed how you live or feel about yourself? Might there be other complementary habits that would also make your life more fulfilled?

....

....

....

Is your life abuzz with positive vibes? Has it changed how you see things?

....

....

....

However the past 52 weeks went, whatever you achieved, acknowledge the good, the less good, and look forward to the hopes and dreams you have yet to fulfil.

....

....

....